Busy Mor... ... .

Daily Devotionals

{Book 1}

By: Lara Velez, Founder of Moms of Faith®

Credits:

Cover Art: canstock.com, cover design by AlibooWebDesign.com

Table of Contents

Introduction

Being a mom means life is busy. We have so many responsibilities, places to go, activities, and things to do. Unfortunately, If we are too busy for God, then we are far busier than He created us to be!

Busy Moms of Faith Daily Devotions are written by me, Lara Velez, a busy homeschooling mom, wife, author, blogger, web designer, and business owner.

I am no stranger to busy and frequently camp out there! Unfortunately, we busy moms, tend to put aside our King!

This should never be!

The daily devotions in this series are tailor made for busy moms! They are designed to take 15 minutes or less each day!

I pray that "Book 1" is the beginning of victory, peace, and hunger for the Lord that no schedule can contain!

How to Use this Devotional

These devotions are written in several parts.

First is the most important. It is the core verse and devotional.

Then, there is your study time, something to chew on, prayer, and journal pages.

On very busy days, make sure that you at least get the core Scripture read and devotional. However, do not make this a habit! The goal should be to do the entire day and the journaling! Altogether it really should take no more than 15 minutes.

In all honesty, and not trying to make you feel guilty, but seriously, God deserves our time! So, if we cannot find 15 minutes to sacrifice for the One who loved us enough to send His Son to pay the price for our sins, maybe--just maybe we need to reevaluate our schedules and priorities!

My Prayer for You

Father God, You are so good. You are more than we could ever hope for. You are so kind and loving. I adore You. You are my love, my King, and my everything! Thank You for each woman reading this. Thank You for her commitment to You and her desire to know You better. Lord, I pray that You meet her where she is at and help her to be the woman that You created her to be. I ask that You bless her time with You each day, and give her a deeper hunger for Your Word. I pray that You bless her abundantly in every area of her life. I declare victory in her life and for every need to be met! I pray a hedge of protection over her and her family as she walks faithfully commits her schedule and time to You. Help her, Lord. Help her to be faithful and committed to her daily time with You. Thank You, Lord. Thank You for helping me write this book, and for the many books that will follow in this series. I pray that these books bless each woman who reads them beyond measure! I love You, Lord. My life is Yours. Use me and mold me into the wife, woman, and mother that You created me to be! In Jesus' Mighty Name, amen!

Day 1: The Lord is My Rock

The Lord is my rock, my fortress and my deliverer; my God is my rock, in whom I take refuge. He is my shield and the horn of my salvation, my stronghold. - Psalm 18:2

If you are alive and breathing then you know how hard life can be at times. None of us are immune to trials. It is a simple fact of life.

The good news is that as Christians, we have something the world does not have, our Daddy God. He is so much more than a Sovereign King who sits high on a throne somewhere. He is a loving God who loves us each individually and profoundly.

This Scripture is just one of the many ways that He expresses and shows His love for us.

Think about it...

He wants us to know that we do not have to go through life on our own. We have a Rock to stand behind. We have a

Fortress to hide under. Daddy God IS our refuge. He is our Shield and will protect us...

IF... we LET Him.

You see, it is all about our will. We have choices in life. One of these choices is whether or not we will TRUST our Lord and Savior. Yes, it requires trust to leave something at His Feet. It requires TRUST to take refuge in His loving arms.

When we are children, we trust our parents... even if they are poor parents. We trust them to take care of us, feed us, comfort us when we are hurt, scare the boogie man away, etc. Well, God is our ultimate parent. He is unfailing and will never let us down like our earthly parents. Who better to put our trust in??

However, the key is that we PUT our trust in God. We must make the decision to trust Him and place whatever storm we are going through at His Feet, and hide in the shelter of His Mighty Fortress!

We can be certain that He will never leave us. He will never harm us. He will never allow us to go through anything that is not for our benefit. Yes, even trials can be for our benefit. They make us stronger and more reliant on Him!

So, the next time a storm comes along and tries to toss you to and fro, hang on to the ROCK!

Study Time:

Look up the following Scriptures and write down at least one thing you feel confirms that God wants us to rely on Him from each.

1 Peter 5:7

Philippians 4:6-7

Psalms 40:1-3

Something to Chew On: Do you struggle with trusting God in a particular area of your life? Think about it today, and then take it to Him, and ask Him to heal that area of your life/thinking.

Core Scripture (meditate on this today): *The Lord is my rock, my fortress and my deliverer; my God is my rock, in* *whom I take refuge. He is my shield and the horn of my salvation, my stronghold. - Psalm 18:2*

Let's Pray:

Father God, thank You for protecting me and providing shelter for me in the storms of life. Help me to trust You and lean on You. Help me to find refuge in Your arms and not let the storm dictate my destiny. I love You, Lord. I love You more than life. You are an Awesome and Mighty God! In YOU I will take refuge... MY Rock! In Jesus' MIGHTY Name, Amen!

Journal...

1 Peter 5:7 Cast all your anxieties on him because he cares for you!

Philippians 4:6-7 Do not be anxious about anything! Let God know your requests, through prayer. Gods peace will guard your heart.

Psalms 40:1-3 Wait patiently and He will hear your cry. He will rescue you and put new song in mouth.

Where do I have problems trusting God?
- Future plans
- Daily stresses
- & Pray about healing!

God is my Rock!
My protector — He has all answers & knows all plans!

Journal...

* whenever have stressful situation, pray for God to guide to correct actions — give it over to him to relieve stress

:D

Day 2: Don't Panic!

So be strong and courageous! Do not be afraid and do not panic before them. For the Lord your God will personally go ahead of you. He will neither fail you nor abandon you." - Deuteronomy 31:6

I am not sure why it is so hard for us to believe that God will not fail us. We certainly all have our testimonies, and times in our lives that we can look back and remember all that He has done to get us through various circumstances in our lives. Yet... we still freak out and panic when things seem to fall apart!

It MUST be a lack of faith! Because, if we believe that God IS, and that His Word is true, and that He cannot lie, then, we would believe He will never leave us, abandon us, or fail us!

We need to trust the One Who will NEVER leave us. We need to remember that this is the same God Who did not spare His Only Son, so that He could be with us. He adores us! We are His baby girls! He has our backs! He WILL personally... PERSONALLY go ahead of us! It says it right there!

So be strong and courageous! Do not be afraid and do not panic before them. For the Lord your God will personally go ahead of you. He will neither fail you nor abandon you." - Deuteronomy 31:6

WOW!

The King of kings will go before me! The Creator of the Universe... the One Who spoke the worlds into existence will PERSONALLY go before me... you ... US!

That makes me want to jump and shout!

Do you get it???

Don't Panic!

Your Daddy in Heaven has your back!

Study Time:

To further drill this into our thick heads, let's look up the
following Scriptures and write them out in our own words, so
we do not forget WHO goes before us!

Psalm 91:1-16

Numbers 23:19

Hebrews 13:5

Titus 1:2

Something to Chew On: What is your biggest fear in life?
Once you know it, release it. Is it bigger than your God?? NO
way! We need to get the right perspective about our fears,
and realize that our purpose goes beyond them. Consider
this: if your worst fear came true, what then? Doesn't your
Father in Heaven still sit on the throne? You would still
survive! Trust Him enough to get you THROUGH anything!

Core Scripture (meditate on this today): *So be strong and
courageous! Do not be afraid and do not panic before them.*

For the Lord your God will personally go ahead of you. He will neither fail you nor abandon you." - Deuteronomy 31:6

Let's Pray:

Father God, thank You for never leaving me and never forsaking me. Thank You for always having my back and always blessing me. You, alone, are worthy of all glory, honor, and praise. I love You, Lord. Thank You for loving me. Help me to remember all the things You have already done for me and to never forget! Lord, I put all my hope and trust in You. I know that no matter what comes my way, you WILL get me through it! Forgive me for ever doubting You! In Jesus' MIGHTY Name, Amen!

Journal...

Psalm 91:1-16 God will protect you!
If you make God your dwelling
place, no evil will befall you
and his angels will protect you.

Numbers 23:19 God keeps promises
and will bless you

Hebrews 13:5
"Keep your life free of money,
and be content with what you
have... I will never leave you
nor forsake you."

Titus 1:2 God promised eternal
life

Journal...

Day 3: Praise be to God!

Praise be to God, Who has not rejected my prayer or withheld His Love from me. - Psalm 66:20

This is AWESOME!!! God will NEVER reject us, He will ALWAYS love us, and He will ALWAYS hear our prayers!

This should be enough to have you dancing in the streets.

Yes, life is hard.

Yes, there are days we want to call it quits.

Yes, there are many trials.

Yes, there is sorrow we must endure.

Yes, there are times we wonder why me, why now, why…

Here's the GOOD news…..

Praise be to God!!!! We are LOVED by the Mighty King. We are LOVED by the Great I AM!!! We are LOVED by the Creator of all things!

And not only are we loved... we are a priority to Him. He takes the time to tentatively listen to our prayers... our cries... our shrieks... He LISTENS!!!!

He will ALWAYS take the time to listen.

Now, that should make your day... your week... no... your LIFE!!!

Study Time:

Look up the following Scriptures and write out the "good news" that each one tells you!

Romans 8:28

Isaiah 40:31

Proverbs 3:6

John 3:16

1 John 1:9

Something to Chew On: Focus on at least 3 things that you can praise God about. When doubts, trials of life, and difficulties come, reflect on the good that your King has already done for you!

Core Scripture (meditate on this today): *Praise be to God, Who has not rejected my prayer or withheld His Love from me. - Psalm 66:20*

Let's Pray:

Father God, thank YOU!! Thank YOU! Thank YOU! Praise You, Lord. You are Worthy of ALL glory, honor, and praise. You are an AWESOME and MIGHTY God! I am humbled by your Great Love for me, and the abundant grace and mercy that You show me each day. Thank You for all that You have done and do for me each day! Thank You for sending Your Only Son so that I can spend eternity with You! I love You, Daddy, God. I just love YOU!!! In Jesus' Mighty Name, amen!

Journal...

Romans 8:28 For those who
love God all things are good.

Isaiah 40:31 Those who wait
for the Lord shall renew
their strength; they shall
mount up with wings like
eagles; shall run and not
be weary; shall walk
and not faint.

Proverbs 3:6 In all your ways
acknowledge him, and he
will make straight your
paths.

John 3:16 For God so loved the
world that he gave his
only son, that whoever
believes in him should not
perish, but have eternal
life.

Journal...

1 John 1:9 If we confess our
sins to him, he is faithful
and just to forgive us our sins
and cleanse us from all
wickedness.

3 Praises:
   Family
   Shelter
   Love

Day 4: Beat a Dead Horse

No, dear brothers and sisters, I have not achieved it, but I focus on this one thing: Forgetting the past and looking forward to what lies ahead. - Philippians 3:13

I have the memory of an elephant. I can tell you who, what, where, how, and why I was hurt or abused… If I let myself dwell on the past. Maybe you don't have the "beat a dead horse" syndrome like me… hey, more power to ya!

I'm speaking to anyone with the following symptoms…

- Holds a grudge.
- Has difficulty letting go of hurts, anger, disappointments, etc.
- Brings up the past in an argument.
- Dwells on the coulda, shoulda, woulda's…
- Lets their mind reflect on the past.
- Can't let go of the past.

If you suffer from one or more of the above symptoms, I have FANTASTIC news! There is a CURE! And guess what?

There are no harmful side affects… well, other than a sore flesh.

THE CURE:

- Step One: Give it to the Father
- Step Two: LET it GO!
- Step Three: Look forward. Press on.
- Step Four: REPEAT until it works!!!
- Bottom Line: LET GO OF THE PAST!

You will NEVER find happiness there. The only thing you will find is anger, pain, and disappointments. Don't keep reminding yourself and others of their past failures. Get OVER it! I'm sorry if this seems abrasive, but it's the Truth. LET IT GO! If you don't YOU will be miserable until you do. YOU will only hurt yourself and those you really love. Release it to your Daddy and LEAVE it there!

It's YOUR choice. You CAN do it…. IF you want to.

Study Time:

Look up the following Scriptures and write them out in our own words, and write out at least one thing from each that encourages you to "stop beating a dead horse"...

Proverbs 3:5-6

Ephesians 4:31-32

Isaiah 43:18-19

Something to Chew On: Do you have a memory like an elephant? How's that working for you? Well, if it hinders your now, not too great. Let go of the past, focus on the now, and set your eyes on the road ahead! You have a race to complete, and your Daddy in Heaven is at the finish line cheering you on!

Core Scripture (meditate on this today): *No, dear brothers and sisters, I have not achieved it, but I focus on this one thing: Forgetting the past and looking forward to what lies ahead. - Philippians 3:13*

Let's Pray:

Father God, thank You for Your Word. Please help me to let go of (you fill in the blank). I no longer want this baggage. PLEASE take it from me and help me to look forward and press on. Please send Your Holy Spirit to remind me to let it go when I try to pick it up again. Thank You, Daddy. I RELEASE it to You. Thank You so much for taking this burden from me. Thank YOU! THANK YOU! Praise You Jesus! Thank YOU! I receive Your Peace, Lord. I receive it. In Jesus' MIGHTY name, amen!

Journal...

* Proverbs 3:5-6 Trust in the Lord with all your heart, and do not lean on your own understanding. In all your ways acknowledge him, and he will make straight your paths.

Ephesians 4:31-32 Put all bad aside. Be kind to one another, tenderhearted, forgiving one another, as God in Christ forgave you.

Isaiah 43:18-19 Remember not the former things, nor consider old things.

Journal...

Let it go!

Day 5: The devil is a Liar!

And I am convinced and sure of this very thing, that He Who began a good work in you will continue until the day of Jesus Christ [right up to the time of His return], developing that good work and perfecting and bringing it to full completion in you. – Philippians 1:6

We must remember this Scripture when we are going through difficult times, feeling down, and when we fail. We are a work in progress. God is not finished yet. He is perfecting and preparing us. And He is FAITHFUL. He will complete His work in us.

When things go wrong or we fail, the enemy just loves to come around and whisper negative things into our heads…

"you'll never get this right… what's wrong with you… you're not good enough… you're fat…. you're ugly… God doesn't really love you… God's mad at you… when will you ever get it right… you're this… you're that… you'll never… you'll always…"

THE devil IS A LIAR!!!

The WORD says that You are a child of God and that He that has begun a good work in you... WILL complete it! The Word says that you are the head and not the tail (Deuteronomy 28:13)... The Word says that you are chosen (1 Peter 2:9)... The Word says that He formed you in your Mother's womb (Psalm 139:13)... The Word says that GOD LOVES YOU (Psalm 103:11-13)... The Word says that the devil is a LIAR (John 8:44)!

Who are you going to believe?

Study Time:

Look up the following Scriptures and write them out in our own words.

1 Peter 5:8

Romans 8:33

Philippians 1:6

Romans 5:1

Something to Chew On: *The devil is a liar! Never forget that he hates your guts! Reflect on this image: Stay alert! Watch out for your great enemy, the devil. He prowls around like a roaring lion, looking for someone to devour. - 1 Peter 5:8*

Core Scripture (meditate on this today): *And I am convinced and sure of this very thing, that He Who began a good work in you will continue until the day of Jesus Christ [right up to the time of His return], developing that good work and perfecting and bringing it to full completion in you. – Philippians 1:6*

Let's Pray:

Father God, You are an Awesome and Mighty God. You are Worthy of ALL the glory, honor, and praise! Thank You for loving me and calling me Your very Own. Thank You for Your life-giving Word. Help me to remember who and Who's I am. Help me to overcome the enemy and his lies with Your Mighty Word. Help me to see his tactics before they take root in my mind. Thank You that You will complete Your Work in me, and that I am a work in progress. Thank You for Your love! In Jesus' MIGHTY Name, Amen!

Journal...

Journal...

Day 6: Unto the Lord

Whatever may be your task, work it heartily, as something done for the Lord and not for men. – Colossians 3:23

If you ever struggle with housework or any job you have as a wife and/or Mother inside or outside the home, this is for you.

If we put our tasks into the right perspective, we will find them easier to do.

There are many tasks that we have as Mothers: cooking, cleaning, grocery shopping, nursing, loving, cleaning, child rearing, drill sergeant, chauffeur, oh… and did I mention cleaning?

For many of us it is a constant struggle just to keep the house decent. Others may find their tasks, meaningless, boring, too much, or unenjoyable.

We can change all of this if we do EVERYTHING for the Lord. If we make it an act of worship, we will find joy in seemingly meaningless duties. If we make the choice to allow God to SHINE in EVERY area of our lives, we WILL be MUCH happier.

Study Time:

Look up the following Scriptures and write them out in our own words.

Proverbs 16:3

1 Corinthians 10:31

Psalm 90:17

Something to Chew On: Being a busy mom can be stressful at times. However, if we focus on the joy of the children God blessed us with, and all the other many blessings God has given us as mothers and women, there is less to complain about! Putting our perspective in the right direction will help us to do our "busy mom" duties with joy, and as unto the Lord, because let's face it, it should be! Our kids belong to Him anyway! Let's make the limited time journey with them enjoyable--by choice!

Core Scripture (meditate on this today): *Whatever may be your task, work it heartily, as something done for the Lord and not for men. – Colossians 3:23*

Let's Pray:

Father God, thank You for the gift of Motherhood. Thank You for ALL that comes with being a Mother... the good and not so good. Thank You for the opportunity to teach my children by example how to live a life dedicated to You. Thank You for loving me and helping me to... (whatever area you struggle in). You know I struggle in this area. You also know that I want my life to reflect You. Help me to find joy in the journey! I love You. In Jesus' MIGHTY Name, Amen!

Journal...

Journal...

Day 7: But If You Do Not Forgive...

For if you forgive men when they sin against you, your heavenly Father will also forgive you. But if you do not forgive men their sins, your Father will not forgive your sins.
— Matthew 6:14-15

This is one of those Scriptures we like to bypass. We don't like to spend too much time examining it. It makes us very uncomfortable. We all have had our share of forgiveness battles. We have all been wronged on some level... some more than others.

We seem to have this need to hold onto our anger and unforgiveness. We even make excuses for ourselves. Unfortunately, none of our reasonings can change the infallible Word of the Living God. Jesus makes it crystal clear: Forgive and be forgiven. Do not forgive and you will not be forgiven.

It's more than John 3:16 and 1John 1:9, sisters. It's about being obedient and giving the same as we are seeking. Why should we be pardoned if we will not pardon an offense? Well, we will not. We must take the words of Christ VERY seriously. We must develop a forgiving heart, and release our hurts and anger to the Lord. We must obey this command. If we do not, then we are playing a game that does not have a happy ending.

Remember this: We are NEVER hurting the offender when we harbor unforgiveness, we are ONLY hurting ourselves!

Study Time:

Look up the following Scriptures and seek God about them. Pray over them, and meditate on them. Let God heal you, teach you, and help you forgive.

Mark 11:25

Ephesians 4:31-32

Matthew 18:21-35

Something to Chew On: Do you struggle with forgiveness? Trust me, I understand! I have been through a lot in my life... sexual abuse, rape, a husband who cheated on me, loss of a child... is it hard to forgive? YES! However, when we realize the price that was paid for OUR sin, how can we NOT forgive another? My sin is no different from your sin. No one is above sin. There are no "sin categories" in the Kingdom. Sin is sin. We must view it from the right perspective: forgive others = receive forgiveness. I do not even want to consider the flip side of that equation! Is it easy? No way! Good news: Daddy is always ready, willing, and able to assist His beloved daughters!

Core Scripture (meditate on this today): *For if you forgive men when they sin against you, your heavenly Father will also forgive you. But if you do not forgive men their sins, your Father will not forgive your sins. – Matthew 6:14-15*

Let's Pray:

Father God, please help me to forgive as I have been forgiven. Please help me to develop in this area. Help me to let go and give it all to You. Forgive me for holding onto anger and bitterness. I release it all to You right now, by faith. I believe that You will set me free as I release it to You. Help me to die to unforgiveness EVERY day. I love You, Lord. And I want nothing to hinder my growth or relationship with You. Thank You. In Jesus' MIGHTY Name, amen!

Journal...

Journal...

Day 8: For a Thousand Generations

Understand, therefore, that the Lord your God is indeed God. He is the faithful God who keeps His covenant for a thousand generations and lavishes His unfailing love on those who love Him and obey His commands. - Deuteronomy 7:9

I love that we serve a God Who is faithful. He does not change with the "times" (Malachi 3:6), or give way to culture and worldly ideals. He just IS (Exodus 3:14). We can be secure in His unending love (Psalm 36:7) and His steady, and unchanging hand over our lives. I don't know about you, but this is gold for me! Considering this crazy ever-changing world we live in, just knowing that the Almighty God is faithful, loves me, and wants to lavish me, gives me more comfort than anything this world has to offer!

He really loves us. His love is so deep and so profound, there are no ways to measure it. It is simply immeasurable.

Understand, therefore...

You, my dear, dear sister, are LOVED... unfailingly loved by an unfailing God Who keeps His promises! You are loved by the One who spoke the sun, moon, and stars into existence. You are adored by the King of kings, and Lord of Lords. You are the precious apple of your Daddy, God's eye (Psalm 17:8, Zechariah 2:8)!

Rest in that TRUTH!

Study Time:

Look up the following Scriptures, write them out in your own words, and reflect on God's faithfulness and steadfastness.

Hebrews 13:8

James 1:17

Lamentations 3:22-24

Psalm 36:5

Something to Chew On: God IS faithful! He will never, ever, ever, EVER leave you. He adores you! If we can just get that into our thick skulls, we would have so much more peace in this life!

Core Scripture (meditate on this today): *Understand, therefore, that the Lord your God is indeed God. He is the faithful God who keeps His covenant for a thousand generations and lavishes His unfailing love on those who love Him and obey His commands. - Deuteronomy 7:9*

Let's Pray:

Father God, I am in awe of You and Your great love for me. My heart sings knowing that the Creator of the Universe loves me, and will never stop loving me. Thank You for being steady, never changing, and Your unending faithfulness. Thank You for never leaving me, and always caring for me. Help me to never forget just how much You love me! Wrap Your arms around me, Daddy God. I want nothing more than to climb up into Your lap, and rest in Your unfailing love! In Jesus' MIGHTY Name, Amen!

Journal...

Journal...

Day 9: God Longs to be Gracious to Us!

And therefore the Lord earnestly waits [expecting, looking, and longing] to be gracious to you; and therefore He lifts Himself up, that He may have mercy on you and show loving-kindness to you. For the Lord is a God of justice. Blessed are all those who wait for Him, who expect and look and long for Him–for His victory, His favor, His love, His peace, His joy, and His matchless, unbroken companionship! – Isaiah 30:18

I used the Amplified Bible translation for this verse, because after I studied the verse, I found that it describes it perfectly based on original Hebrew text. However, I still want to look at the word gracious. It comes from the Hebrew word chanan and means: bend in kindness to an inferior; to favor, bestow, give, grant, and be merciful.

I love this!

Isn't it amazing to think that GOD… The King of kings and Lord of lords earnestly WAITS and LONGS to be gracious to us??? He wants to bestow kindness and favor on us. No– He WAITS and LONGS to do it! It is His desire to bless us.

He is not some angry god somewhere in the sky that does not care for us. He is the ONLY True God, and He loves each of us so profoundly, that He actually deeply desires to love us, and show us kindness, mercy, and favor. He wants to help us through His Word, and the petitions of our prayers through faith and give us: peace, joy, and unbroken– matchless companionship!!!

This Word has set a fire under me to press on and fight the battle before me! I will not cower and miss the blessings and victory that my Daddy in Heaven has for me! Nope! This girl is getting armed and opening her arms to the mercy, grace, and love that my–OUR God so freely wants to give!

Study Time:

Look up the following Scriptures, pick the 3 that speak the most to you, write them out in your own words, and keep them with you!

1 Peter 5:7

Isaiah 41:10

John 14.13-14

Proverbs 10: 6

Jeremiah 29:11

Isaiah 40:29-31

Nahum 1:7

Something to Chew On: Do you realize just how much you are loved and adored by the Creator of the Universe? If not, what do you think hinders you from grasping that Truth? I want you to really think about this. Ask God to help you find the source of your doubt, then lay it at His feet, and grasp the reality of just how profound His love is for YOU!

Core Scripture (meditate on this today): *And therefore the Lord earnestly waits [expecting, looking, and longing] to be gracious to you; and therefore He lifts Himself up, that He may have mercy on you and show loving-kindness to you. For the Lord is a God of justice. Blessed are all those who wait for Him, who expect and look and long for Him—for His victory, His favor, His love, His peace, His joy, and His matchless, unbroken companionship! – Isaiah 30:18*
Let's Pray:

Father God, thank You for never leaving me! Thank You for putting people into my life that speak Your Word and Truth over me. Thank You that I can find help, encouragement, and weapons for warfare in Your Word. I love You, Lord, and I want to live victoriously. I am amazed that You, the Creator of all things, longs to do anything for an unworthy peasant like me. I am in awe of Your great love for me! Here I am, Lord, opening my heart and arms to the grace, mercy and blessings that You have for me! I receive them, in Jesus Name, I receive!! Thank You!! In Jesus' MIGHTY Name, Amen!

Journal...

Journal...

Day 10: When You are Feeling Overwhelmed

O God, listen to my cry! Hear my prayer! From the ends of the earth, I cry to You for help when my heart is overwhelmed. Lead me to the towering rock of safety, for You are my safe refuge, a fortress where my enemies cannot reach me. Let me live forever in Your sanctuary, safe beneath the shelter of Your wings! – Psalm 61:1-4

He IS our safe refuge. He DOES hear us. We ARE safe beneath the shelter of His wings.

Yes, I will face trials and troubles in this life, and yes, I may feel overwhelmed at times. However, I know that I know that I KNOW my God loves me, and will NEVER leave me or forsake me–no matter how dark and dreary it gets!

Be strong, courageous, and firm; fear not nor be in terror before them, for it is the Lord your God Who goes with you; He will not fail you or forsake you. – Deuteronomy 31:6

I hope that this encourages you as much as it did me. Never forget that God loves you, and cares for you right in the middle of the lowest of your muck--and the high points as well!

Study Time:

Look up the following Scriptures, pick one that speaks the most to you, write it out in your favorite translation, and put it where you can see it regularly.

Psalm 119:105

Romans 5:3-5

Matthew 19:26

James 1:2-4

Something to Chew On: When do you find yourself feeling overwhelmed the most? OK, now that you know, keep this in mind: it is OK. God is with you, and He wants to walk WITH you! Climb up on His lap and let Him help you!

Core Scripture (meditate on this today): *O God, listen to my cry! Hear my prayer! From the ends of the earth, I cry to You for help when my heart is overwhelmed. Lead me to the*

towering rock of safety, for You are my safe refuge, a
fortress where my enemies cannot reach me. Let me live
forever in Your sanctuary, safe beneath the shelter of Your
wings! – Psalm 61:1-4

Let's Pray:

Father God, forgive me for wallowing in a sea of self
pity and forgetting that I am the daughter of the
Most High. Forgive me for forgetting that You are with
me and that WITH YOU, I CAN face any storm, and
that You, the Creator of the Universe, will be with me
every step of the way. I love You, Lord. Thank You for
loving me! In Jesus' MIGHTY Name, Amen!

Journal...

Journal...

Day 11: Always Near

The Lord is righteous in all His ways and gracious and merciful in all His works. The Lord is near to all who call upon Him, to all who call upon Him sincerely and in truth. He will fulfill the desires of those who reverently and worshipfully fear Him; He also will hear their cry and will save them. – Psalm 145:17-19

I find this passage of Scriptures to be profoundly comforting when I am in the muck of self pity. I am reminded that the Creator of all things, the King of kings, the Great I AM is ALWAYS near me. He loves me and NEVER leaves my side. If I ever feel distant, it is not because HE is not there, it is because I am not seeking...

It is because I forget that He not only loves me and bestows abundant mercies on me daily, He also HEARS me and SAVES me when I cry out to Him!

You see, there are times that Daddy must save us from US! He must grab us from the pits of our own minds and inner fears. The devil cannot be blamed for everything. Many times it is our own flesh and sinful nature that we must be saved from.

Oh, how glorious it is to be HIS–the Almighty God, Who wants us to call Him Abba (Daddy), loves each of us so profoundly and considers us HIS very own. HE will not let anything snatch us from His love–and we should not allow our own doubts, fears, sin and pains to turn us from the ONLY ONE who TRULY loves us, and will fight FOR us!

Study Time:

Look up the following Scriptures, and read them out loud.

Matthew 7:7-8

1 John 5:14-15

Psalm 46:1

Psalm 55:22

Matthew 11:28-30

Isaiah 43:1-3

John 16:33

Something to Chew On: Can you feel a theme over the past few days? I think God wants us to understand how much we are loved! Take time to meditate on the core Scripture and those that spoke the most to you in your homework today!

Core Scripture (meditate on this today): *The Lord is righteous in all His ways and gracious and merciful in all His works. The Lord is near to all who call upon Him, to all who call upon Him sincerely and in truth. He will fulfill the desires of those who reverently and worshipfully fear Him; He also will hear their cry and will save them. – Psalm 145:17-19*

Let's Pray:

Father God, thank You for loving me and calling me Your very own. Thank You that I am YOUR daughter. Help me to see You and seek You in the midst of my pain and trials I need You, Daddy I cannot even breathe without Your help. Never let me go! In Jesus' MIGHTY Name, Amen!

Journal...

Journal...

Day 12: Let all that I am Praise the Lord

Let all that I am praise the Lord; with my whole heart, I will praise His holy name. Let all that I am praise the Lord; may I never forget the good things He does for me. He forgives all my sins and heals all my diseases. He redeems me from death and crowns me with love and tender mercies. He fills my life with good things. My youth is renewed like the eagle's! - Psalm 103:1-5

Man, I just LOVE my Daddy God. He is so worthy of all my praise! He is awesome, mighty, wonderful, fabulous, loving, kind, worthy, glorious, merciful, giving, slow to anger, King of kings, Lord of lords, the Great Physician, my Strong Tower, my Provider, my Redeemer, my Savior, My Beloved, my Friend…the LOVE of my life!!!!

I want my life to be filled with His praise, and for my light to shine brightly! Let ALL that I am PRAISE HIS HOLY Name!!!!

He redeems me!!!!

He forgives me!!!!

He heals me!!!!

He loves unworthy me!!!!

He really loves me…just as I am!!!!

He gives me good things!!!!

He shows me mercy ALL the time!!!!

Let us NEVER forget His goodness, love and mercy! Not even for a second!

WE LOVE YOU, LORD!!!!

Study Time:

Memorize our Core Scripture.

Something to Chew On: Today, we need to really dwell on these 5 Scriptures. Repeat them until they sink in!

Core Scripture (meditate on this today): *Let all that I am praise the Lord; with my whole heart, I will praise His holy* *name. Let all that I am praise the Lord; may I never forget the good things He does for me. He forgives all my sins and heals all my diseases. He redeems me from death and crowns me with love and tender mercies. He fills my life with good things. My youth is renewed like the eagle's! - Psalm 103:1-5*

Let's Pray:

Father God, thank You for love. I love You and want my life to bring glory to Your Name. Let all that I am PRAISE Your Holy Name. You are Worthy of all glory, honor and praise! Thank you for loving me, Daddy! In Jesus' MIGHTY Name, Amen!

Journal...

Journal...

Day 13: Even Our Enemies...

When a man's ways please the Lord, He makes even his enemies to be at peace with him. - Proverbs 16:7

At first glance, we may miss something. However, if we take a minute to think about what this verse is saying, we may be surprised!

If we live our lives for the Lord, we know through His Word that there are MANY promises we can and will receive. However, this is an amazing promise of peace...

...He makes even his enemies to be at peace with him.

It is hard enough to remain in peace with our loved ones, spouses, friends, co-workers, and sisters & brothers in Christ. Yet, if our lives are lived for the Lord, and our walk (because of our obedience) is pleasing to Daddy God, EVEN OUR ENEMIES will be at peace with us!

I find this to be incredible!

Living in peace with ANYONE can be difficult if you are in relationship with them for a long period of time. To have the kind of peace mentioned in this Scripture would be fantastic!

However, as with all of God's promises, there is a "doing" on our part. Obedience is required. We must CHOOSE to live for Him, and obey His precepts. Not only for the promises, but because of our love and appreciation for all that He is, and all that He did and does for us! How could we NOT want to walk with our Lord and submit our lives to Him??

Study Time:

Look up the word "peace" and find five Scriptures that speak to YOUR circumstances. Write them out, meditate on them and dig deeper.

Something to Chew On: Can you imagine having the kind of peace in your relationships like what is mentioned in Proverbs 16:7? It is amazing to me how God knows just what we need! He understands that peace is needed--even with our enemies. All that is required to get it is to honor our God, and walk with Him--because as we do, we will desire what He desires, and obedience will surely follow. He is not asking for perfection--that is what Jesus came for. All He wants is a willing heart, and His daughters to seek Him and walk with Him!

Core Scripture (meditate on this today): *When a man's ways please the Lord, He makes even his enemies to be at peace with him. - Proverbs 16:7*

Let's Pray:

Father God, thank You for Your Word. Thank You for the promises that Your Word holds for me. Thank You for all that You are, all that You do for me every day, and all that You have done for me. Thank You for the sacrifice of Your Son so that I may have right relationship with You, and walk in victory! I love You, Daddy! In Jesus' MIGHTY Name, Amen!

Journal...

Journal...

Day 14: A Harvest of Joy

Those who plant in tears will harvest with shouts of joy. They weep as they go to plant their seed, but they sing as they return with the harvest. - Psalms 126:5-6

This is such an amazing promise to me. To be completely honest, there are many days I feel like this will never come to pass. So, I have to remind myself often that God's Word does not lie--and that even though it has not happened yet–I KNOW it will!

I have wept many tears in my marriage–in life. I have often cried out to God in frustration and demanded to know WHY. I think it is natural to get sick and tired of being sad; or in a place of despair; and to see no light at the end of the long, dark tunnel we have been in. I do not think God gets mad when we cry out to Him. However, I think we need to make sure (and I am preaching to me as well) that we remember WHO is in charge, and that God works ALL things for our good.

I have planted a vineyard of tears!! I am so ready to reap my harvest of joy!!! How about you?

Study Time:

Look up the following Scriptures, and read them out loud.

Romans 12:12

Philippians 4:4

James 1:2

Nehemiah 8:10

Psalm 16:11

Something to Chew On: Have you planted tears in your life?? Well, get ready for the joy, dear sister! 'Cause it is coming for you!

Core Scripture (meditate on this today): *Those who plant in tears will harvest with shouts of joy. They weep as they go to plant their seed, but they sing as they return with the harvest. - Psalms 126:5-6*
Let's Pray:

Father God, thank You for Your Word, and the Truth it holds. I thank You for my tears, and that You have even found a way to bless me in my sorrows! Please give me strength on this journey, and hold me up when I am too weak to go on. I love You, Lord. In Jesus' MIGHTY Name, Amen!

Journal...

Journal...

Day 15: Close to the Brokenhearted

The Lord is close to the brokenhearted; He rescues those whose spirits are crushed. - Psalm 34:18

Life is hard--for some, harder than others. We get our hearts broken, or we just become crushed over time simply from the trials of life. That is why I love this promise!

My Daddy in Heaven is always close to me! When my heart is broken, He is right there, ready to mend it. When my spirit is crushed by the hardships of life, He is there to rescue me! He will not let me be consumed. He loves me. He loves YOU!

If we will just have faith to believe God's Word, and trust Him enough to DO what He says, then this promise is ours for the taking! God will never leave us. Never! We need to take our hurts, pain, disappointments, and brokenness to Him, and let Him heal us, restore us, and love on us.

Seriously, all Daddy wants to do is care for us.

We are His baby girls!

All we need to do is grasp this truth, and reach out for the life vest!

Study Time:

Look up the following Scriptures, and read them out loud.

Psalm 147:3

Matthew 11:28

Revelation 21:4

Isaiah 41:10

Something to Chew On: I think one of the hardest things for us to grasp with our human minds is just how much God loves us. We must understand that He actually wants to comfort us. He wants to love on us. He created us to love Him, so that He can love us back! Take some time today as you go through your busy day, to think about all that God has done for You. Focus on all the many blessings that you have. Can't you see? The King of kings LOVES you!

Core Scripture (meditate on this today): *The Lord is close to the brokenhearted; He rescues those whose spirits are crushed. - Psalm 34:18*

Let's Pray:

Father God, thank You for never leaving me! Help me to trust You, and reach for You in my times of need and brokenness. I want to climb up in Your lap and just let You love on me. Thank You for caring for me so deeply. I love You, Daddy. In Jesus' MIGHTY Name, Amen!

Journal...

Journal...

Day 16: Stop Being Stubborn

The Lord chose your ancestors as the objects of His love. And He chose you, their descendants, above all other nations, as is evident today. Therefore, change your hearts, and stop being stubborn. - Deuteronomy 10:15-16

Make no mistake, my dear sister, you and I are chosen. We are grafted into this promise (Romans 11:7) by the precious Blood of our Savior, Jesus Christ. We were chosen before the foundations of the earth (Ephesians 1:4). Being chosen by the Almighty God is an amazing feeling. Knowing that He loves us so very much and that He chose us--even knowing all the mistakes and junk that would come with us... He STILL chose...

Stop being stubborn.

Knowing how He feels about us. Knowing His great love for each of us. Knowing all that He has done, is doing, and will do for us...

Knowing all of this should be enough to cause us to rid ourselves of stubbornness, and DO what He called us to do.

Knowing all of this should help us to live obedient lives. Knowing all this should make us desire to be all that He created us to be.

So, rather than make excuses, let's just...

Stop being stubborn!

Study Time:

Look up the following Scriptures, and write them out in your own words.

John 14:15

1 Peter 1:20

James 1:14-15

1 Peter 2:9

Something to Chew On: Any time we read Scriptures that urge us to stop sinning, obey, or "stop being stubborn", we tend to want to throw out Scriptures about "freedom", "forgiveness", and "saved by Grace"... And, all of that is well and good. However, our salvation is not a license to sin. We should never be so comfortable in our sin that we throw the Blood back in God's face. We need to turn FROM sin and stubbornness, turn TO God, and walk in obedience. *(ref. Romans 6:23; 1 John, chapter 3; 1 Corinthians 10:13; Galatians 6:7-9)*

Core Scripture (meditate on this today): *The Lord chose your ancestors as the objects of His love. And He chose you, their descendants, above all other nations, as is evident today. Therefore, change your hearts, and stop being stubborn. - Deuteronomy 10:15-16*

Let's Pray:

Father God, thank You for loving me and saving me. Forgive me for any willful sin in my heart. Forgive me for being stubborn at times, and not begin quick to obey You. Thank You for always having my best in mind. I love You, Lord. Help me to never forget the price that was paid for my salvation. Help me to never walk in habitual sin. Thank You. In Jesus' MIGHTY, Loving, and Saving Name, Amen!

Journal...

Journal...

Day 17: A World Filled with God's Righteousness

But we are looking forward to the new heavens and new earth He has promised, a world filled with God's righteousness. – 2 Peter 3:13

I look forward to the day that I get to be in Heaven with my King. This Scripture is so very encouraging. Sure, I love being a mom and my life here on earth. However, it lifts my soul to know that I have a promised home after this earthly life ends that will be filled with God's love, and have no sin, pain, sorrows, or loss. That is what all of His children have to look forward to!

So, on those days when life is getting the better of you, and you wonder how you will make it through, remember that you have a promise from the King. A promise of a wonderful eternity overflowing with joy!

We cannot allow this life to break us down! We must lay hold of the promises of God, and walk in the knowledge of what lays ahead of us!

Study Time:

Look up the following Scriptures, and write them out in your own words.

Romans 8:28

Joshua 1:9

John 14:2

Revelation 21:4

Something to Chew On: It's easy to get caught up in the "here and now", and forget we are but aliens here. We tend to live life with fleshly eyes, rather than through the eyes of our spirit. If we would open our hearts and minds to the Truth of God's Word, we would find that our lives are overflowing with promise! We HAVE a wonderful future! We will be with our King forever! If we can grasp that, then we can find more joy in THIS life! Live on purpose, ladies!

Core Scripture (meditate on this today): *But we are looking forward to the new heavens and new earth He has* *promised, a world filled with God's righteousness. – 2 Peter 3:13*

Let's Pray:

Father God, Thank You for providing a future for me filled with hope, joy, and abundance. Thank You that I have Heaven to look forward to at the end of my days here on earth. Help me to lay hold of that promise and find joy in the here and now! Help me to live this life with purpose and with the knowledge that it is for but a fraction of my existence. Help me to be thankful for each day with my children, and to enjoy this life You have blessed me with! In Jesus' MIGHTY Name, Amen!

Journal...

Journal...

Day 18: So Good, So Ready, So Full...

*O Lord, you are so good, so ready to forgive, so full of
unfailing love for all who ask for your help. - Psalm 86:5*

I have always loved David. He paints such an incredible
portrait of our King, and it is not based on fiction, it is based
on David's actual experiences with Almighty God!

So Good...

Think about all the ways our Daddy in Heaven is Good! He
protects us (ref. Psalm 91), guides us (ref. Proverbs 3:5-6),
loves us (ref. Romans 8:37-39), forgives us (ref. 1 John 1:9),
saves us (ref. John 3:16), heals us (ref. Psalm 103:3)... and
so much more that there are not pages enough to fill with the
Goodness of our God!

So Ready...

He does not hold a grudge! When we fall flat on our faces,
He is ever ready to forgive us. When we walk completely
away from Him, He is lovingly waiting for us with arms wide
open! Of course, He does not want us to live in sin, but He is

always ready to forgive us when we repent! He is awesome like that!

So Full...

Our King is faithful and full of unfailing love for us! He wants to help us! He is always listening and always available when we need Him. Isn't that amazing?? He is never ever, ever unavailable!

Study Time:

Look up the following Scriptures, choose the one that speaks to your current season in life, write it out, and memorize it!

2 Thessalonians 3:3

Psalm 32:8

Romans 5:8

Isaiah 43:25

Ephesians 2:8

1 Peter 2:24

Something to Chew On: I think we forget just how much God loves us, how much He cares for even the littlest thing in our lives, and how much He wants to be involved with our day-to-day lives! Never forget just how "full" of grace, love, mercy, forgiveness, provision, help, mercy, and goodness Your God is! He adores You, and wants nothing more than to pour out His love on your life! You have a faithful God, Who will NEVER leave you! Let Him take care of you--His baby girl!

Core Scripture (meditate on this today): *O Lord, you are so good, so ready to forgive, so full of unfailing love for all who ask for your help. - Psalm 86:5*

Let's Pray:

Father God, You are so good and faithful. I am overwhelmed by Your great love for me! Help me to remember just how much You love me! Thank You so much, Lord. Thank You for Your forgiveness, mercy, grace, and goodness in my life. Thank You for your faithfulness. Thank You for never leaving me! I love and adore You, my King! You are Holy! Holy and Worthy is Your Name, Father. In Jesus' MIGHTY Name, Amen!

Journal...

Journal...

Day 19: But Those Who...

Even youths will become weak and tired, and young men will fall in exhaustion. But those who trust in the Lord will find new strength. They will soar high on wings like eagles. They will run and not grow weary. They will walk and not faint. - Isaiah 40:30-31

This is one of my many favorite Scriptures. Our God is just so amazing and awesome! He has so many promises for His beloved children!

But Those Who...

Trust.

Trusting the Lord may seem like a no-brainer, but do we really trust Him--with everything? Do we trust Him with our money and tithe? Do we trust Him with our ears and eyes, and allow the Holy Spirit to help us decide what to watch? Do we trust Him with our kids?

Do we really trust Him in ALL things?

I would venture to guess, no. Each of us have our own struggles in our walk, and our biggest sin struggles can be traced back to trust.

How can we NOT trust our King! His Word tells us just how trustworthy He really is:

- He will NEVER leave us (Deuteronomy 31:6)
- He cannot lie (Hebrews 6:18)
- He IS love (1 John 4:8)
- He is faithful (Deuteronomy 7:9)
- He KEEPS His promises (Numbers 23:19)
- He loves you and nothing can change that! (Romans 8:38-39)
- He is just (Psalm 7:11)
- His mercy and goodness are forever (Psalm 23)
- He just... well... IS (Revelation 1:8)

Study Time:

Look up the following Scriptures, and be encouraged!

Psalm 25:8-14

2 Peter 3:9

Titus 1:2

Psalm 103 (whole chapter)

Something to Chew On: Trust your Daddy in Heaven, and He will give you NEW strength! You will soar! You will run and not grow weary! You will NOT faint! How do I know this? Because His Word says so, and our God cannot lie!

Core Scripture (meditate on this today): *Even youths will become weak and tired, and young men will fall in exhaustion. But those who trust in the Lord will find new strength. They will soar high on wings like eagles. They will run and not grow weary. They will walk and not faint. - Isaiah 40:30-31*

Let's Pray:

Father God, thank You for being faithful! Thank You that I know that I know that I KNOW that I can trust You! Thank You for never leaving me, and for Your never ending love for me. Help me to trust You in ALL ways, Lord. Show me how! Forgive me for not trusting You in every area of my life. Lord, in the areas that I am less than faithful, I ask that You teach me how to be faithful. I love You, Lord, and I want to live a life that brings glory to Your Worthy Name! In Jesus' MIGHTY Name, Amen!

Journal...

Journal...

Day 20: You are Beautiful!

I praise you, for I am fearfully and wonderfully made. Wonderful are Your works; my soul knows it very well. - Psalm 139:14

Unfortunately, being a woman in this sex crazed, skin showing, unrealistic, outward beauty obsessed world can make even the prettiest woman feel like a wall flower!

Well, it is time for a self-esteem booster, my dear sister!

You were made by the Almighty God!

You are beautiful! He made you, and God does not make mistakes. He is the ultimate artist! If you look at the planets, and the world around you, it is clear that He is pretty good at what He does!

Some of us are pleasantly plump, some tall, some short, some thin, some white, some dark. It matters not! We are made by the Creator of the universe, and should NEVER measure our beauty and worth by the world's standards!

Study Time:

Look up the following Scriptures, and write them out in your own words!

      Ephesians 2:10

      Psalm 100:3

      Job 33:4

      Isaiah 64:8

      Job 31:15

I would also like to encourage you to read Psalm 139 in its entirety when you get some time. It will encourage you!

Something to Chew On: You are beautiful! If you doubt that, take it up with God, 'cause you would be wrong, my dear!

Core Scripture (meditate on this today): *I praise you, for I am fearfully and wonderfully made. Wonderful are your works; my soul knows it very well. - Psalm 139:14*

Let's Pray:

Father God, it is so hard to see myself as beautiful. Everywhere I look with my flesh eyes, I see much prettier than me, and then I read how YOU made me, and how You were there forming me in my mother's womb. Oh, Daddy, forgive me for not seeing the beautiful woman in the mirror. Forgive me for criticizing Your handiwork! I love You, Lord. Thank You for creating me! Help me to see me the way I REALLY am-- beautiful! In Jesus' MIGHTY Name, Amen!

Journal...

Journal...

Day 21: The Darkest Valley

Even when I walk through the darkest valley, I will not be afraid, for You are close beside me. Your rod and Your staff protect and comfort me. - Psalm 23:4

Anyone alive and living on planet earth has or soon will walk through at least a few "dark valleys" in their lives. It is a part of life. As Christians, we are not promised a "trouble free" existence. However, we do have something that the world does not: a Daddy in Heaven Who never leaves us, and walks WITH us... and even carries us through our valleys!

We need NOT be afraid! He is close to us. His Word is what will aid and comfort us. It will also provide protection!

How?

Well, as we read His Word, we learn what His Will is and the authority His Word gives His children. There is comfort, peace, and power within its pages--all we have to do is read it and apply it!

Study Time:

Look up the following Scriptures, then choose the two that encourage/help you the most, write them out in your own words and keep them close!

Hebrews 4:12

Colossians 1:13

1 Corinthians 10:13

Isaiah 40:31

Hebrews 13:6

Something to Chew On: God's Word tells us in Hosea 4:6 that we (His people) are destroyed for "lack of knowledge". If we refuse to gain "true knowledge" that can only be found in His Word, we are heading for destruction--whether it be physically, relationally, spiritually, or financially. We must not use ignorance as a crutch. It will not save us from harm. We must read God's Word and gain true knowledge, pray, and be diligent. When we do this, we are better equipped *(ref. 2 Timothy 3:16-17; 1 Peter 5:8; Psalm 119:105)*, able to walk in victory *(ref. Philippians 4:13; James 1:12-14; Ephesians 6:13)*, and we will be properly positioned under the protection of the Almighty *(ref. Psalm 91:1-3; 2 Samuel 22:3-4; Psalm 121:7-8)*!

Core Scripture (meditate on this today): *Even when I walk through the darkest valley, I will not be afraid, for You are close beside me. Your rod and Your staff protect and comfort me. - Psalm 23:4*

Let's Pray:

Father God, thank You for Your Word. May I never take it for granted. Lord, please forgive me for spiritual apathy. Help me to set my eyes on You and Your purposes for my life. Help me to understand that this world is but a fraction in my eternity. Help me to know You better, Lord. Please make Your Word come alive every time I read it! Lord, I ask that You bless this time I spend doing these mini devotionals every day. Help me to be diligent and apply all that I learn!

Lord, forgive me for not making You a priority in my life! I love You, Daddy. Thank You for loving me! In Jesus' MIGHTY Name, Amen!

Journal...

Journal...

Day 22: School Yard Pick

Furthermore, because we are united with Christ, we have received an inheritance from God, for He chose us in advance, and He makes everything work out according to His plan. - Ephesians 1:11

It always brings tears to my eyes, and warmth to my heart, when I hear that God "chose me in advance". You see, I was that kid that no one chose for their team in the infamous "school yard picks". So, for me, knowing that He actually CHOSE me is amazing! Dear, sweet, sister, He chose you too! He knew every sin, and icky part of what our hearts would be, and still chose us!

Here's the real kicker though, not only did He choose us; He also has an inheritance for us. We are joint heirs with Christ *(ref. Romans 8:17)*! We are royal princesses *(ref. 1 Peter 2:9-10)*!

As if that was not fabulous enough... He makes everything work out. We may not always understand His plan, but we know that if God is the one with the plan, it will go far better than anything we can come up with!

Study Time:

Look up the following Scriptures, and write them out in your own words!

Galatians 3:26

John 1:12

Ephesians 2:10

Something to Chew On: I want to reiterate that we (that includes you) are royalty! We are princesses of the King of kings! If we would realize our position and grasp just WHO our Daddy is, we would find ourselves with a lot more peace, joy, and victory! Note: Make sure that you look up the Scriptures above and all reference Scriptures in today's study.

Core Scripture (meditate on this today): *Furthermore, because we are united with Christ, we have received an inheritance from God, for He chose us in advance, and He makes everything work out according to His plan. - Ephesians 1:11*

Let's Pray:

Father God, thank You for choosing me! Thank You for
loving me! I cannot imagine my life without You. Help me
to never forget just how much You love me, and that I
am your royal princess. Help me to teach my children
that they were also chosen to be your princes and
princesses! Thank You for all that You are, Daddy. I
love You! In Jesus' MIGHTY and Loving Name, Amen!

Journal...

Journal...

Day 23: Not Even the Powers of Hell!

And I am convinced that nothing can ever separate us from God's love. Neither death nor life, neither angels nor demons, neither our fears for today nor our worries about tomorrow—not even the powers of hell can separate us from God's love. No power in the sky above or in the earth below—indeed, nothing in all creation will ever be able to separate us from the love of God that is revealed in Christ Jesus our Lord. - Romans 8:38-39

Sometimes in life we mess up--big time. It is during those times, we may think God is mad at us, has given up on us, or that we have somehow lost His love. Well, that is simply not true. It is a lie from the pit of hell to keep us away from climbing up into our Daddy's loving lap.

The Truth is: NO power in hell or of any kind can separate us from God's love. No mistake, wrong thinking, worries, person, demon, or anything else can stop your Daddy in Heaven from loving you! NOTHING!

You are the apple of His eye *(ref. Zechariah 2:8)*!

Study Time:

Look up the following Scriptures, choose the two that speak to you the most, write them out in your own words, and keep them close at hand!

Romans 5:8

Psalm 36:5

Revelation 3:19

1 John 4:9-10

Psalm 26:3

Something to Chew On: We will never be perfect. God knew that before He ever created us and called us. That is why He sent us Jesus! However, I do want to make sure I say something: nothing can separate us from the love of God, but that is not license to live in willful sin. We must make sure that we are repentant when we sin, and are walking out our salvation with fear and trembling *(ref. Philippians 2:12)* -- Meaning, that we take the Blood seriously, and do not take our forgiveness for granted *(ref. Galatians 6:7)*!

Core Scripture (meditate on this today): *And I am convinced that nothing can ever separate us from God's love. Neither death nor life, neither angels nor demons, neither our fears for today nor our worries about tomorrow— not even the powers of hell can separate us from God's love. No power in the sky above or in the earth below—indeed, nothing in all creation will ever be able to separate us from the love of God that is revealed in Christ Jesus our Lord. - Romans 8:38-39*

Let's Pray:

Father God, thank You for Your love. Thank You that nothing I do can ever stop You from loving me. I am amazed by You and Your faithfulness to me! I love You, Daddy. Help me to never take for granted the high price that was paid for my Salvation. May I never forget the precious and innocent Blood that was shed for me! Help me to walk Your path for me, and to repent quickly when I stray and sin. I love You, and want my children to see me walk with You all of my days! Help me, Lord. Thank You! In Jesus' MIGHTY and Powerful Name, Amen!

Journal...

Journal...

Day 24: What's In Your Heart?

You brood of snakes! How could evil men like you speak what is good and right? For whatever is in your heart determines what you say. - Matthew 12:34

I love how Jesus just tells it like it is! He is not some wishy-washy weakling. He is Mighty, and when He walked this earth, He called it like He saw it!

His words in this passage can really sting the flesh.

For whatever is in your heart determines what you say...

Oh, Lord, keep evil far from me! This really is a matter of the heart. If we are speaking meanly, negative, rudeness, making crude jokes, slander, cuss words, etc., etc., etc.; it is coming from the depths of our hearts! We must clean out our hearts, so that we can reset our minds, so that we can purify our mouths!

May we never be a brood of snakes!

Study Time:

Look up the following Scriptures, and write them out in your own words.

Proverbs 27:19

Matthew 6:21

Ephesians 4:29

Proverbs 3:5-7

Something to Chew On: We need to take a heart inventory. Think about how you have been speaking lately. Have you been pretty negative? A sour puss? Swearing a lot? Yelling at the kids? Participating in crude jokes? Many times what comes out is a result of what has been going in. Pay attention to what you are watching, reading, and listening to! Regardless of its origin, whatever your heart issue is that is spewing from your lips, repent! Take it to the feet of the Father, repent, and leave it there! Get in the Word, and replace the ick that has accumulated in your heart! Then, you will see the overflowing of God's love and tenderness flowing from your lips!

Core Scripture (meditate on this today): *You brood of snakes! How could evil men like you speak what is good and right? For whatever is in your heart determines what you say. - Matthew 12:34*

Let's Pray:

Father God, forgive me for allowing myself to let my guard down! Forgive me for letting my heart be deceived and filled with junk. Help me to find the origins of my heart issues, and turn from them! Help me to replace the sick portions of my heart with the Truth and healing of Your life-giving Word! Lord, forgive me for anything and everything I have said up to this moment that was not pleasing to you. Help me to shut my mouth more, listen more, and pray more! I love You, Lord. Thank You for Your forgiveness, strength, and help! In Jesus' MIGHTY Name, Amen!

Journal...

Journal...

Day 25: A Priceless Treasure

Your Word is a lamp to guide my feet and a light for my path.
- Psalm 119:105

His Word really is all we need. No amount of money, fame, possessions, fun, wonders for the eyes, or even relationships can compare to what God's Word is.

It is our life line.

It is a love letter from our King.

It is our guide for life on planet earth.

It is healing for our weary souls.

It is our comfort and peace.

It is the light for our path, and the only way to find the right direction.

And SO MUCH more!

Let's read it every day, because honestly, nothing is more important. Nothing.

Study Time:

Look up the following Scriptures, read them out loud, and memorize the one that speaks to your heart the most.

2 Timothy 3:16

Matthew 24:35

Colossians 3:16

Proverbs 4:20-22

Hebrews 4:12

Something to Chew On: Your God is the Almighty God, the Creator of the Universe, Alpha and Omega, the First and the Last, King of kings, and Lord of lords. He IS, and was, and is to come! He is all of that and so much more, and He did not leave You without a precious living part of Him: His Word. It is vital to our lives, and we should not only read it often, we should keep it on hand, and know it well!

Core Scripture (meditate on this today): *Your Word is a lamp to guide my feet and a light for my path. - Psalm 119:105*

Let's Pray:

Father God, thank You for Your Word, and the life within its pages. Thank You for leaving me a piece of You. Thank You for leaving me a guide for my life. Help me to crave it. Help me to read it, learn it, and bury it deep in my heart. I love You and Your Word, Lord. Thank You for the love letter that You left me, and the priceless treasure that it is for my life! You are amazing and wonderful, Father! I love You. In Jesus' MIGHTY Name, Amen!

Journal...

Journal...

Day 26: Oh, the Joys

Taste and see that the Lord is good. Oh, the joys of those who take refuge in Him! - Psalm 34:8

Our God is so good. There is none like Him! Oh, the joys of those who take refuge in Him! I don't know about you, but I would love some more joy in my life! Wouldn't you??

I looked up the original Hebrew text for "refuge" from this verse and found the following:

It comes from chacah (khaw-saw'), and means: to flee for protection, to confide in, have hope, make refuge, (put) trust.

This really brought it to life for me! You see, when we put all of our trust and hopes in the Lord, we are taking refuge in Him. When we confide in Him and trust Him to protect us, we are taking refuge in Him.

And, when we take refuge in the Most High, we will be blessed, happy and overflowing with joy!

I mean seriously, who can hold a candle to our King?

Study Time:

Look up the following Scriptures, read them out loud, write out the one that speaks to your heart the most, and keep it in your Bible.

Psalm 9:10

Psalm 62:8

Romans 15:4

1 Peter 5:7

Psalm 46:1

Romans 12:12

Something to Chew On: The amazing thing about being a child of God is that we do not have to "go it alone". He is always with us and ever faithful. All that is required of us is to follow Him, trust Him, and put our hope in Him. He will help us, protect us, and honor His Word and the promises that it holds! He is trustworthy, and desires to give us joy! He WANTS us happy, healthy, and safe! He WANTS us living victorious lives! We must take refuge in Him and His Word, and learn who we are, and what we are promised!

Core Scripture (meditate on this today): *Taste and see that the Lord is good. Oh, the joys of those who take refuge in Him! - Psalm 34:8*

Let's Pray:

Father God, thank You for Your promises. Thank You for the promise of JOY! Oh, how I love Your Word! Thank You for giving it to Your children! Thank You for only wanting the best for me. Thank You for always having my back, and never leaving me. Thank You for Your faithfulness and love. Thank You for Your forgiveness and mercy. Lord, please help me to train my heart and mind to trust in You, and not what I see with my human eyes. I need Your Word to come alive in my heart, and for You to teach me how to live. I love You, Lord. Thank You for loving me! In Jesus' MIGHTY Name, Amen!

Journal...

Journal...

Day 27: Commit Your Work...

Commit your work to the Lord, and your plans will succeed. - Proverbs 16:3

Whether you are a stay-at-home mom, a work-at-home mom, or one that works outside the home, every mom works. We all have desires that we want to succeed, and dreams of something we would love to accomplish.

No matter what it is--even something as seemingly meaningless as getting a handle on housework, commit it to the Lord.

Lay everything you do down at His feet. Give Him all of your hopes and dreams--both big and small!

When we do this, we are opening the door so that God can fulfill His promise.

Study Time:

Look up the following Scriptures, read them out loud, and then write them out in your own words.

Colossians 3:23

Psalm 37:5

Jeremiah 26:14

Something to Chew On: I want to make sure that I point out that our plans cannot be born from sin, or from selfish ambitions. Obviously, if we are walking with the Lord, and are in a "committed" relationship with Him, our plans and work will ultimately line up with His will for our lives. However, if we are not walking with Him, and have strayed, we may be deluded into a wrong mindset. So, make sure that your plans line up with God's Word, and that You are always including God in every decision--both big and small!

Core Scripture (meditate on this today): *Commit your work to the Lord, and your plans will succeed. - Proverbs 16:3*

Let's Pray:

Father God, you never cease to amaze me! Thank you for the many promises that your Word holds for me.

May my plans never veer away from Your will for my life. I pray that You only allow desires to rise up in my heart that are pleasing to You. Lord, I ask that You make my deepest dreams come true. I ask that You help me with the works of my hands, and to prosper in all that I do. I pray that everything I put my hand to will bring glory to Your Worthy Name! I love You, Daddy. Thank You for loving me! In Jesus' MIGHTY Name, amen!

Journal...

Journal...

Day 28: Perfect Peace

You will keep in perfect peace all who trust in You, all whose thoughts are fixed on You! - Isaiah 26:3

Just reading this verse at face value excites me! However, I dug deeper and looked up the original Hebrew for the word "peace" in this text and what I found was awesome!

It comes from the word shalowm (shaw-lome') and means; safe, well, happy, health, prosperity, favor, rest, peace, wholly.

Wow!

God is so incredible! I mean He loves us so much, and has so many great things that He wants to bless us with; and PERFECT PEACE is one of them!

When we focus on Him, make Him a priority in our lives, and include Him in our lives; He promises to protect us, prosper us, keep us safe, well, happy, and healthy--wholly!

Are you dancing yet??

Study Time:

Find 3 Scriptures using any of the following words: peace, safety, happy, prosper. Choose the one that speaks to you the most, write it out in your favorite translation, and refer to it as needed!

Something to Chew On: God only wants to do good in our lives. He wants to bless us, prosper us, and keep us in perfect peace. All He wants in return is for us to love, trust, and follow Him. How can we not want to follow the One Who will never leave us or forsake us, and Who loves us like no one else ever could? Let's commit to make God the top priority in our hearts, minds, and lives--and not just somewhere on a long list of things we need to do each day!

Core Scripture (meditate on this today): *You will keep in perfect peace all who trust in You, all whose thoughts are fixed on You! - Isaiah 26:3*

Let's Pray:

Father God, You are so Good! You are faithful and kind. I am in awe of all that You are and all that You want to bless me with. Thank You for the promise of perfect peace. Thank You that it is available to me as I fix my thoughts on You. Thank You for always providing for me and never leaving me. Thank You that I can fully trust You and never be disappointed. Thank You for all that You are to me. You are everything to me, Daddy, and I adore You! Thank You for loving me so profoundly! In Jesus' MIGHTY and Loving Name, amen!

Journal...

Journal...

Day 29: "Do Not Fear; I Will Help You!"

For I am the LORD your God who takes hold of your right hand and says to you, Do not fear; I will help you. - Isaiah 41:13

I am going through a huge financial trial right now. It has been a real test of my faith. Sure, I can throw out a few Christian clichés, and act as if I am not struggling. But, what good would that do?? I have been called to be open and honest with you.

That being said, even in the midst of our greatest difficulties, we need not fear.

Why?

Well, it says it right there in Isaiah 41:13: Because God WILL help us. It may not be the way we want Him to, or at the time we think it should happen, but we can rest assured that He WILL help us!

How can I be so sure?

He said so, and God cannot and does not lie! Period.

Study Time:

Look up the following Scriptures and read them out loud.

Exodus 14:14

Proverbs 3:5-6

Psalm 118:7

Isaiah 41:10

Psalm 30:10

Something to Chew On: God will never disappoint. Sure, we may not get everything our flesh desires; however, we can rest in the knowledge that we serve a King Who does not leave His people without aid!

- He WILL supply our needs. (ref. Philippians 4:19)
- We will not be forsaken or need to beg for bread. (ref. Psalm 37:25)

- He has a good plan for us. (ref. Jeremiah 29:11)
- He will protect us. (ref. Isaiah 41:10 & Isaiah 54:17)
- He is faithful! (ref. 2 Thessalonians 3:3)

Core Scripture (meditate on this today): *For I am the LORD your God who takes hold of your right hand and says to you, Do not fear; I will help you. - Isaiah 41:13*

Let's Pray:

Father God, sometimes it is hard to understand what Your plan is. Right now, I am struggling. Please help me to trust You with my finances (insert your area of lacking trust if different from mine). I know that You are trustworthy, You have proven Yourself time and time again in various areas of my life. My spirit knows this is no different. Help my mind to catch up with my spirit! Thank You, Daddy! Thank You for Your Word, and for the promise of helping me! Lord, I am calling out to You now! Help me! In Jesus' MIGHTY and Loving Name, amen!

Journal...

Journal...

Day 30: Whatever Is...

Finally, brothers and sisters, whatever is true, whatever is honorable, whatever is just, whatever is pure, whatever is lovely, whatever is commendable, if there is any excellence, if there is anything worthy of praise, think about these things.
- Philippians 4:8

I believe that every sin we commit began in our mind. What we think about greatly affects what we will do, say, believe, and put into action.

What we allow to take up residence in our minds will ultimately lead us to abundant life or sadly, death--whether spiritually, physically, financially, or even relationally.

We need to set our minds on what is good!

We need to think about what is pure, lovely, and praiseworthy, and kick the negativity to the curb!

Study Time:

Look up the following Scriptures and read them out loud, choose one that speaks the most to you, write it out in your own words, and memorize it!

Romans 12:2

1 Corinthians 6:19-20

Romans 8:5-6

2 Corinthians 10:3-5

Something to Chew On: We must be mindful of what we allow to gain access to our thought life. Anything that goes in will inevitably come out in some form. If we read trash, watch trash, and listen to trash, well then, trash is what will take up space in our heads, and manifest itself as sin one way or another. We must not be apathetic! We need to hold every thought captive, and submit everything we do to the Lord. We need to pay attention to what we are doing, and the entertainment that we give countless hours of access to our minds!

Core Scripture (meditate on this today): *Finally, brothers and sisters, whatever is true, whatever is honorable, whatever is just, whatever is pure, whatever is lovely, whatever is commendable, if there is any excellence, if there is anything worthy of praise, think about these things. - Philippians 4:8*

Let's Pray:

Father God, forgive me for allowing trash to take up residence in my mind. Forgive me for watching, reading, and listening to anything that is not pleasing to You. Help me to pay closer attention to what I am allowing to enter my thought life. Teach me Your ways, Lord. Show me where I am lacking and what I need to let go of. I love You, Lord, and I want my life to please You! I do not ever want to do anything that would taint Your name to those that I influence. In Jesus' MIGHTY name, amen!

Journal...

Journal...

Final Thoughts

I want to encourage you to keep pressing into God's Word. Go through this devotion again, or get another one! The point is: do not stop spending time with your King every day!

FYI: Book 2 in this series is coming soon.
Visit: Facebook.com/BusyMomsofFaith
And like our page to remain updated on future devotionals in this series!

God Bless You!

Note: keep reading for resources and more! There are also a few extra journal pages at the end of the book.

Encouragement for Moms

This book is only the beginning of the support and encouragement we have for you!

Moms of Faith *(momsoffaith.com)* is an awesome website tailor-made for Christian moms. You will find resources, tips, helpful articles, spiritual growth topics, and so much more for moms like you!

Weekly Encouragement Email for Moms: Sign up to receive a weekly devotional, encouragement, resources, and more for Christian moms... *http://eepurl.com/w6EtH*

Private Facebook Group for Moms. *(facebook.com/groups/momoffaith)* Christian Moms coming together to support, pray, and encourage one another! We also have a powerful prayer meeting each month!

Are you married?

There is encouragement for you too!

Real Christian Wives *(realchristianwives.com)* is a powerful website for wives; with monthly challenges, prayers, spiritual growth topics, and so much more. There is also a great tool located on this site. Look for the tab, "30 Day Prayer Journey for Wives" for a powerful prayer study.

Weekly Encouragement Email for Wives: *Sign up* to receive a weekly devotional, encouragement, support, and more for Christian wives... *http://eepurl.com/Fq_fj*

Proverbs 31 Wife Handbook:
(proverbs31wifehandbook.com) An easy to follow daily devotional explaining how to be a "Proverbs 31 Wife" in today's culture. This book was written for any wife who wants to have a better marriage, be the wife that God designed them to be, or is desperate for a change. **We also have a work-at-your-own-pace web class that goes with the book.** When you visit the site, look for "web class" in navigation for more info.

Private Facebook Group for Wives.

(facebook.com/groups/RealChristianWives) Purpose: To offer a place for Christian wives to come and learn, grow, read relatable content from REAL wives like them, and find support. We are here to be REAL with our readers; and to share our good, bad, ugly, and everything in between. We also have powerful monthly prayer meetings in there!

About the Author

Lara is a wife, mom, homeschooler, published author, ministry leader, speaker, and supreme multi-tasker! She is honest and forthright in her writing, and shares her heart, struggles, joys, pains, and the many lessons she has learned on her journey–in a relatable way that pulls no punches.

Besides all that, she is a chauffeur, friend, maid, chef, business owner, lover, confidant, mentor, teacher, seeker, nurse, boo-boo kisser, cat lover, coffee drinker, Starbucks follower, Mexican food addict, jean loving, sometimes loud mouth, opinionated, outspoken, web designer, iphone carrier, a teensy bit anal retentive, chocoholic, Survivor fan, Bible believing, animal lover, reptile and crawly things hating, speed walking, honest, working her way back to skinny jeans, and… One heck of a strong woman! (Among other things)

Subscribe to Lara's mailing list to stay updated on current book, specials, book signings, speaking engagements, and more here: **http://eepurl.com/w0asT**

You can find her:

LaraVelez.com

Facebook.com/LaraVelez.Author

Twitter: @Faithful_Mommie

More books by her...

Proverbs 31 Wife Handbook

Fruit of the Spirit Series

Psalm 91: He Who Dwells (study into the PROMISE of protection)

And many more!

"O God, listen to my cry! Hear my prayer! From the ends of the earth, I cry to You for help when my heart is overwhelmed. Lead me to the towering rock of safety, for You are my safe refuge, a fortress where my enemies cannot reach me. Let me live forever in Your sanctuary, safe beneath the shelter of Your wings!" – Psalm 61:1-4

Journal...

Journal...

Journal...

CPSIA information can be obtained at www.ICGtesting.com
Printed in the USA
LVOW04s1836290415

436596LV00032B/853/P

9 780991 539311